Travels with Grace

by Erma Note

Illustrated by Ileana Pérez-Monroy

Halo
PUBLISHING
INTERNATIONAL

ISBN: 978-1-61244-668-4
Library of Congress Control Number: 2018909541

Printed in the United States of America

Halo Publishing International
1100 NW Loop 410
Suite 700 - 176
San Antonio, Texas 78213
1-877-705-9647
www.halopublishing.com
contact@halopublishing.com

This book is dedicated to my three, beautiful daughters: Isabella, Siena, and Juliana. The character of Grace is based on all three of these intelligent, worldly travelers. May you always learn, grow, and explore. I love you with all my heart.

To Serafin: Thank you for your support and for joining me on our journey.

To Lisa and Halo: Thank you for encouraging me to write and giving me the tools to make this dream a reality.

To Lynda: Thank you for sharing your time and expertise. You have taught me so much about Mexico.

To Sandra: Your perfectionism is exquisite.

To Mom: You were the one who instilled in me the confidence to travel the world by myself from a young age. Without your guidance, I would never have had the courage to spread my wings and fly. I know you are guiding me from Heaven.

Foreword

"Travel is fatal to prejudice, bigotry, and narrow-mindedness, and many of our people need it sorely on these accounts. Broad, wholesome, charitable views of men and things cannot be acquired by vegetating in one little corner of the earth all one's lifetime."

- Samuel "Mark Twain" Clemens

Una Visita (A Visitor)

Grace is nine years old. She lives in Mexico City. Grace's mom is from the United States of America, and Grace's dad is from Mexico. That means that Grace is bicultural—she is both *mexicana* (Mexican) and *estadounidense* (American). Grace was born in Mexico City. It is a huge city of more than 20 million people. That is a lot of people! Grace speaks *inglés* (English) and *español* (Spanish). When she speaks with her mom and her English teacher at school, Grace speaks in English. When she speaks with her dad, her friends, and people in the store, Grace speaks *en español*. That means that Grace is bilingual—she speaks two languages.

El Itinerario (The Itinerary)

Grace's mom's family members all live in Chicago. Grace is excited because her *primo* (cousin), Connor, is coming to visit from Chicago for the first time. Grace loves traveling and hosting visitors. She enjoys showing visitors all around Mexico City.

"Grace, I need your help," says Mom.

"Sure, Mom, what do you need?"

"I need you to help me plan for Connor's visit so that we can show him new and interesting things in Mexico City," Mom replies.

Grace and Mom sit down at the kitchen table to think of places to take Connor during his visit to Mexico City. They make a list, which can also be called an itinerary.

El Aeropuerto (The Airport)

On Saturday, Dad and Grace pick up Connor at the Benito Juárez International Airport in Mexico City. Grace gives Connor a big hug because she is happy to see him.

Grace is very excited. She says, "Welcome to Mexico! *¡Bienvenido a México!*"

Then Dad takes Connor and Grace to a *taquería* (taco restaurant), and they eat *tacos al pastor*, or meat tacos. Tacos are a popular food in Mexico. They are usually corn *tortillas* filled with seasoned meat. Some people add onion, cilantro, spicy *salsa*, and other toppings to their taco.

"Delicious!" exclaims Connor.

"*¡Qué sabroso!*" says Grace.

La Casa Azul (The Blue House)

On Sunday, the family goes to *La Casa Azul* (The Blue House) which was once the home of the famous Mexican painter, Frida Kahlo. The house is a vivid cobalt blue, which is Grace's favorite color. There is a long line of people to get in, but Grace doesn't mind.

Inside, Grace tells Connor a bit about the life of Frida Kahlo.

"Frida was in a bus accident when she was young, and she was badly injured. When she was getting better, she had to lie in bed in a body cast for nine months," says Grace.

"Poor, Frida!" exclaims Connor.

"But she didn't just lie there feeling sorry for herself," Grace tells him. "Oh no! Her parents put a mirror over her bed, and Frida started painting self-portraits. She had a lot of pain and suffering during her life because of her injuries from the accident, but she never stopped painting and living her life. That is what I admire about her: she never gave up."

"I love the colors in these paintings. I have never seen anything quite like this," says Connor.

"Is anyone up for ice cream or *nieve*?" asks Mom.

"I AM!" shout Grace and Connor in unison.

Las Pirámides (The Pyramids)

On Monday, Grace's family takes Connor to visit *Teotihuacán*. It is an ancient site with three huge pyramids near Mexico City. Grace likes to climb to the top of the biggest pyramid —the Pyramid of the Sun— with her family. From there, Grace can see for miles and miles around. Grace's mom likes to wait at the bottom of the pyramid because she is afraid of heights. But Grace is not afraid. She climbs quickly and surely to the very top of the pyramid like a brave explorer!

"Whoa, I feel kind of dizzy!" says Connor. "This is really tall!"

"I know," says Grace. "It's normal to feel a little dizzy all the way up here. Have you ever seen a pyramid before?"

"I have only seen them on television and in a book about Egypt," says Connor.

"Isn't it cool that this pyramid is only a four-hour plane ride away from your home? And I bet you've never stood on a building that is over a thousand years old," says Grace.

"That's true! I never thought about that," says Connor as a warm breeze flutters his shirt. "Now can we climb the Pyramid of the Moon?"

"Of course!" exclaims Grace. "Let's go!"

El Castillo (The Castle)

On Tuesday, Grace and Mom take Connor to Chapultepec Park. The word *Chapultepec* means "at the grasshopper's hill." It is a huge, beautiful park in the middle of Mexico City with lots of trees, a lake with paddle boats, a zoo, and a castle. It is the only royal castle in the Americas, and it is very old. Grace imagines that she is a princess living in a castle when she visits Chapultepec Castle. But now the castle is a museum, and Grace shows Connor all the fancy furniture and paintings that make it look like a setting from a fairy tale.

Connor's favorite part is the murals. A mural is a large painting on a wall. Chapultepec Castle has a lot of colorful art painted by famous Mexican muralists such as David Alfaro Siqueiros and José Clemente Orozco that show representations of Mexico's history—its revolution and journey toward independence.

"It is so colorful and there are so many things to look at," says Connor.

"These murals are helpful to understand Mexico's history," says Grace.

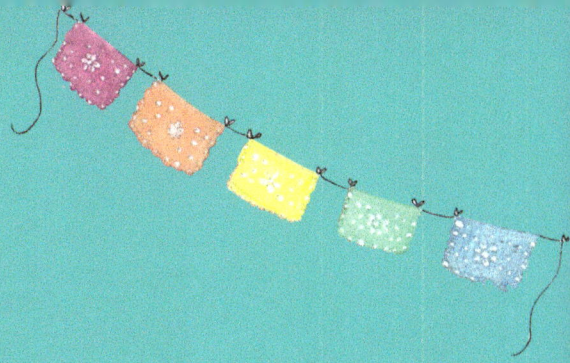

El Museo (The Museum)

On Wednesday, Grace and her family take Connor to see the Soumaya Museum. It is a new museum that was built when Grace was a very little girl. Grace used to say to her mom, "It's MY museum," and Mom would take Grace to see the art in the museum's collection when she was only two years old. The outside of the museum is made of shiny, silver metal, and it reminds Grace of a tidal wave. Inside the museum is an immense collection of art. Grace's favorite piece is a sculpture by Rodin called *The Thinker*.

"We were just learning about Rodin's sculptures in art class," says Connor.

"And now you can see some of them in-person," says Grace. "How neat is that?!"

El Zócalo (The City Center)

On Thursday, Grace and her family take Connor to downtown Mexico City. There are cars and busses everywhere, and there are more people than Connor has ever seen in his life. They see people dancing in the Zócalo, or main square, in interesting outfits with feathered headdresses. They play drums and burn incense. Nearby, Grace, Mom, and Connor enter the Metropolitan Cathedral of Mexico City.

"There's a pyramid underneath the Cathedral," says Grace. "The Cathedral was built on top!"

Connor has never seen such a large church in his life with so many beautiful decorations.

Next, Mom, Grace, and Connor visit the ruins of another pyramid that was uncovered in 1978 by some people that worked for the power company.

"The *Templo Mayor* was considered the center of the universe by the *Mexica* people who founded the city of *Tenochtitlán* hundreds of years ago," says Mom.

Connor says, "I bet that's how the country of Mexico got its name."

"That's a great observation," says Mom.

They walk through the site and admire the sculptures and some paintings that are still visible.

El Mercado (The Market)

On Friday, Mom takes Grace and Connor to the Ciudadela Market. This is a famous market for handicrafts, or *artesanías*, in Mexico City. Handicrafts are made by many local artisans. They make them by hand, rather than using machines. Connor wants to buy gifts for everyone back home to tell them about Mexico. Grace helps Connor choose a *lucha libre* mask for his dad. *Lucha Libre* is professional wrestling in Mexico. The wrestlers wear unique, colorful masks. They buy a lovely handmade *rebozo*, or shawl, for his mom and a *Talavera* ceramic plate for his teacher, Ms. Burke. *Talavera* is a kind of traditional, hand painted pottery that is usually blue and white. It can take weeks to create just one piece of *Talavera* pottery. Grace suggests a beautiful, very colorful embroidered dress for Connor's sister, Clare.

"There are so many amazing things to buy. Everything is so colorful, beautiful, and unique! I hope that everyone likes their gifts," says Connor.

"I am sure they will," Grace reassures him.

Connor Regresa a Casa (Connor Returns Home)

It is Saturday, and today Connor is going back home to his family in Chicago. Grace feels sad. But before they leave for the airport, Dad makes a delicious breakfast of *huevos a la mexicana*, which are scrambled eggs with tomato, onion, green pepper, a bit of garlic, salt, and pepper.

"*¡Qué rico!*" exclaims Connor, licking his lips and reaching for a corn *tortilla*.

"Hey! You're picking up some real Spanish," says Grace. "Good work! *¡Bien hecho!*"

"Well, I have to learn more Spanish so that next time I visit, I will be fluent and can talk to everyone *en la Ciudad de México*," Connor says.

"Great idea," says Grace. "I love having visitors!"

Discussion questions:

Where do you live?

Which language(s) do you speak?

How many people live in your city or town?

Do you like to have visitors? Why or why not?

What are three things that you would show a visitor that came to visit you?

Are there any cities you would like to visit? If so, which ones?

Do you own any handmade things? If so, what are they?

www.ingramcontent.com/pod-product-compliance
Lightning Source LLC
Chambersburg PA
CBHW040851100426
42813CB00015B/2777